Shenandoah Vestiges
What the Mountain People Left Behind

by Carolyn and Jack Reeder

The Potomac Appalachian Trail Club
118 Park Street S.E.
Vienna, VA 22180

ISBN 0-915746-14-X
Library of Congress Catalog Card Number: 80-81761

10 9 8 7 6

Other books about the Shenandoah National Park by authors:

Shenandoah Secrets: The Story of the Park's Hidden Past
Shenandoah Heritage: The Story of the People Before the Park

For more books from the Potomac Appalachian Trail Club on Shenandoah National Park, please check our web site:

www.patc.net

or ask for a publication catalog by calling: 703/242-0315
or by E-mail: patcsales@erols.com

Reprinted in 2017

Cover Photo: Aaron Nicholson homesite, ca. 1976

Shenandoah Vestiges

Years have passed since corn and cabbages grew in Shenandoah. The open land where cattle grazed is forest now. We sometimes forget that generations of people lived out their lives in the mountains we visit for recreation and renewal.

The careful observer, though, can find vestiges of the mountain people and their way of life in Shenandoah National Park—farm sites, tools and utensils, graves, and subtle signs in the forest itself. For though time and vegetation have obscured much of the human history of Shenandoah, a century and a half of habitation cannot be completely erased. Man left his mark here as he struggled for survival.

Acknowledgements

Our thanks to Len Wheat, who helped us find the abandoned homesites and overgrown cemeteries of the mountain people, and to Bessie Compton Woodward and others who helped us better understand the significance of the vestiges we found.

Shenandoah Vestiges:
What the Mountain People Left Behind

Notice

Please leave the scattered discards of the mountain people for future visitors to enjoy. Park authorities state that disturbance or removal of artifacts from the site is a violation of federal law.

Part I

The Sites

The Sites

"How did you happen to get interested in that sort of thing?"

My husband Jack and I hear this question from almost everyone who learns that our hobby is searching for the long-abandoned homesites and cemeteries in Shenandoah National Park. And there are hundreds of homesites and scores of cemeteries hidden in the Park's forests. Shenandoah was inhabited for more than 150 years before the land was taken over for a park.

Our hobby got its start when hiking on the established trails became boring to our children. To create some new interest we decided to explore one of the faint abandoned trails we had noticed. Before long we saw a patch of green on the level forest floor and found a neatly rocked-in spring, then rows of rocks in a rectangular outline— the foundation of a cabin! When one of the children found a rusted-out dishpan and called it an artifact, we were hooked.

No longer bored, the kids accompanied us along abandoned roads and grew quick to spot the apple trees and fence remnants that meant we were nearing a site. Their sharp eyes spotted plowshares and cow bells hidden among layers of dead leaves. Their patient fingers assembled bits of pottery into nearly complete crocks or jugs.

For several years our family outings took us to the Park to ramble and explore far from the trails that other hikers used. But too soon the kids were bored again. Politely, they told us they'd rather spend the weekends in town with their friends.

"Why don't you invite a friend to come with us?" I asked.

"Mom, how many of my friends do you think would want to drive 2½ hours each way to walk through briars in hopes of finding some piles of rocks and rusty old stuff?"

A fair question.

But Jack and I had a friend who would love to do just that! Len Wheat, a fellow member of the Potomac Appalachian Trail Club, had long made solitary bushwhacks across the Park and was familiar with a network of old roads. He began to join us on some of our expeditions.

It must have been about the time our hobby changed from a family activity to an adult activity that "collecting cabins and cemeteries" became an end in itself instead of a diversion. We got organized. Instead of driving to the Park, finding a likely looking old road to follow, and keeping our eyes open for the possibility of a cabin site, Jack and Len did some homework. They used old maps and records to locate houses in the Park area, transferred that information to our PATC hiking maps of the Park, and planned our approach to specific sites.

As we purposefully walked toward the destination site of our day's hike I took careful notes (sometimes through two layers of mittens), and at the site Jack photographed cabins and artifacts. Len, for whom hiking is an activity unhampered by the paraphernalia and delays of record keeping, would wait with good-humored patience.

We named each site we found after some distinctive feature or artifact. There was a Persimmon Tree Site, Vat House, Well House, Seven Springs Site, Toy Farm. . . . But before long it wasn't enough to find the sites; we wanted to know who had lived there.

By reading an old hiking guide that directed hikers to pass So-and-So's cabin and turn left by So-and-So's barn, I was able to identify some sites. Early hiking maps were a help, too, since they showed the cabins of a few mountain families.

And then we made some contacts with people who had once lived in the Park area.

"Who lived in the first house on the right just east of the gap?"

"Why, that was George Herring's."

"And who lived in the next house down the road and across the creek?"

"Just a minute now, and let me think on it. . . ."

The more we learned, the more we wanted to know. On rainy weekends Jack and I pored over photographs and records in Park archives. Besides helping us identify some of our sites, this provided leads to where we could look for others. Even more important, our research gave us a feeling for the people whose homesites we were finding and a sense of history of a type that eludes the textbooks.

So that first chance ramble along an abandoned trail led to a hobby which grew into an avocation. Late fall through early spring we save our weekends for exploring sites. This creates problems with our social life: when a hike is scheduled for Saturday, we don't want to be out late on Friday; we're ready for a long, hot bath and a quiet evening after hiking all day, which takes care of Saturday night. That should leave Sunday, but we usually reserve it in case our hike is rained out on Saturday.

Why do we do it? Certainly not just "because it's there." The challenge is part of it, of course. Our desire to preserve something of the history of the sturdy mountain people who have been either maligned or forgotten is a significant motivation, too. But more selfishly, we also do it because it is something unique that we share, something we can work on together that takes us away from the routine and frustrations of daily life to another time as well as another place.

Most of the old homesites in Shenandoah are marked only by foundation outlines or a mound of chimney rubble, although sometimes you can find standing houses and cabins in various stages of deterioration.

Squared logs shaped at the end for a solid fit, mud chinking, and a dry-set stone chimney were common features of the mountain cabin.

Hand-rived shingles cover this partially standing house.

Inside, you can see marks of the broad ax used to square the logs, traces of plaster still embedded in the walls, and the support for a stairway to the loft. (Out of sight, a piece of hardware from a shade hangs above one window.)

15

Above: *Part of this house has collapsed, leaving only the chimney standing. It was an example of a "double house" or "tandem house" in which a duplicate structure was built a few feet away from the original cabin and joined to it by continuing the new roof across an open "dog trot" or breezeway. The later addition still stands, though the mud chinking is gone.* **Right:** *Without the use of mortar, the mountain mason built chimneys that still stand tall and straight. He chose and laid his stones with care, depending on the force of gravity to hold them in place.*

Many of the people in the Blue Ridge learned first-hand what energy-conscious Americans are being told today: that the fireplace is an inefficient heat source. In some cabins the fireplace has been walled shut, leaving only a hole for the stove pipe to enter the chimney.

Picket fences hewn from chestnut often surrounded cabin yards. Stone fences marked off gardens or fields. Split rail fences, barbed wire strung between chestnut posts, or commercially made woven wire farm fence marked property lines or kept livestock from straying onto roads.

Farmsites usually had several outbuildings. Barns, sheds, chicken houses, meat houses, spring houses, and corn cribs were common; sometimes there was a blacksmith shop, a winery, or a separate kitchen.

This outbuilding, just a few feet from the house, was a kitchen.
   "Some farms had a kitchen house for canning and preserving, washing clothes, and making soap. The messy work was done in the kitchen house, and they cooked there in hot weather."
   Notice the construction details visible here: vertical strips over the logs providing a base for the siding; the frame of the cellar door; the foundation pier at the corner in the foreground; and the ends of the ceiling beams that can be seen above the narrow window.

Lean-tos or sheds were often added to houses and barns. Native shingles cover the addition to this log barn.

Many sites have the remains of a rock-lined root cellar or "vegetable dugout." These were usually built into a slope and covered with a gabled roof.

The spring house provided a cool place to store perishables in warm weather. This one was well built: tight chinking with wedges of wood kept the cool air in and the varmints out.

Most mountain families dipped their water from springs, though a few depended on nearby streams. Some springs flowed naturally from beneath a tree or boulder, but usually they were improved by rocking in the sides and covering the top. When the land was cleared, a tree or a small grove often was left to shade the spring.

Occasionally you will find a site with a rock-lined well. Usually a well was covered by a boxed wooden platform with a hand pump to raise the water. Sometimes the well was under the porch floor and the pump was conveniently near the kitchen door.

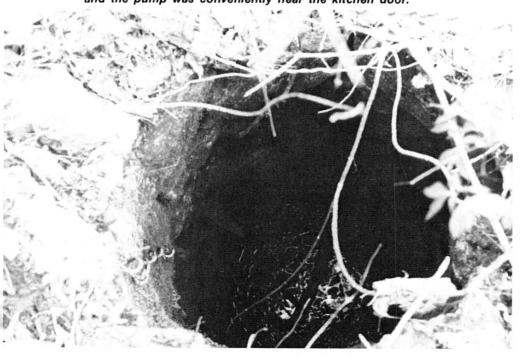

Too much water can be as great a problem as too little water. Mountain farmers dug channels, built diversionary earthen berms, or laid drain tiles to reclaim marshy land.

To prevent undercutting and erosion after heavy rains, one mountain man walled in the bank of a stream where it made a horseshoe bend as it flowed through his land.

At one homesite, forked branches support the cross pieces of an arbor. Grapes were grown throughout the Park area, and some farmers in the northern section made and sold wine.

What excitement you feel when you come upon a mill site deep in the wilderness! The race, two stone piers, and the mill stones are all that is left of this old grist mill.

The heavy millstones represent days and days of tedious work: "If a man needed a millstone, he would hunt till he found him a rock big as he wanted. Then he'd work it level—with a hammer and pick he would work it. When he got it level and round and the hole through it, then he'd go back with a bag of small steel picks and would get it absolutely level and mark the channels out. It would take six months for each stone. They'd use a sled to get it out and a wagon to take it to the mill."

Only a corner of this old mission church still stands.
The Episcopal Church had home missions scattered through the Blue Ridge to provide religious services, education, and other needed services for the local people. Shoes and clothing that had been collected for the mission field were sold at nominal prices because many mountain people were too proud to accept charity.

Part II

Artifacts

Artifacts

When guests pick up one of our photo albums, they're in for a surprise. Instead of family groups and vacation scenes they find tumbled-down cabins, stone chimneys, broken crockery, and strange metal objects.

These albums are part of our research project on Shenandoah National Park's old homesites. Jack photographs what is left of the homes and belongings of the people who lived there before the Park was established. Some of the artifacts in his pictures are clearly recognizable as parts of wood stoves, kitchen utensils, or farm implements. Others are difficult to identify—sometimes because the wooden parts have decayed, sometimes because the object is one that present-day city dwellers are unfamiliar with.

Identifying these artifacts has become a spin-off activity of our explorations in the Park. Museums and living history exhibits helped us identify both the step to a buggy and a wagon brake mechanism. A book on antique kitchen utensils identified an apple peeler. A paperback on antique farm implements pictured another find: a cream separator. Old catalogs helped us determine that one of our photographs showed part of a cider press, another the base of a kerosene heater. Older relatives recognized parts of early vintage autos and a piece of the pulley mechanism that raised a well bucket.

We now understand why archaeologists study artifacts to learn about the people who once lived in an area. The artifacts that are sometimes scattered about the yards of the abandoned homesites in Shenandoah give a picture of the lifestyle of the people who lived there in the 1920s and '30s: woodstoves, washtubs, and chamber pots; crocks for food storage and two-quart mason jars for homemade brandy or corn liquor as well as for putting up garden produce; kitchen utensils that varied from cast iron to enamelware to aluminum; plows, hoes, and mattocks to farm the rocky ground;

wagons, buggies, and cars in areas with decent roads.

A few of the things we've found help dispel the myth that the mountain people lived in poverty: a perfume bottle; bits of decorative glassware and good quality china; parts of Singer sewing machines; the works of a fine clock.

We look through our albums often. Abandoned cabins and broken or rusted artifacts may seem strange subjects for a photo collection, but they call to mind a variety of experiences we've shared while exploring in Shenandoah. And it's pretty satisfying to be developing our own archival records of the daily life of the people who lived in these mountains fifty years or more ago.

Like this spade, artifacts are often well-camouflaged on the forest floor.

At a time when "level landers" were rapidly converting to tractors, the mountain man used hand tools and—if he was fortunate—a horse-drawn plow to farm his land.

Farmers used scythes for mowing hay and harvesting grain.

The two-man cross-cut saw made wood cutting a companionable job. Felling large trees, sawing cordwood for fuel, and readying logs for the sawmill required the use of this tool.

This adz was handwrought from a single piece of iron.
A blacksmith shop was part of some of the larger, self-sufficient farms in the Park area, and smiths were located along the transmountain roads, as well.

Gears operated the mountain man's cornsheller, his grindstone, and his cane mill for making sorghum.

Turning this massive handle operated a cider press similar in design to some of those still sold today.

Shoemaking was a household craft in the nineteenth century. Later, store-bought or cobbler-made shoes were repaired at home using lasts like this one.

This cast iron cauldron, more than a yard in diameter, may have been used for boiling laundry, for making soap, or for rendering lard. It probably rested on several large rocks so that a fire could be built beneath it.

Some mountain families used kerosene space heaters. (The chimney of this one is missing.)

Imagine transporting a stove this size along the footpath to one of the remote mountain cabins!

This iron kettle once steamed on a mountain woman's wood stove.

*The apple peeler was an important utensil for the people in the
Blue Ridge. They used it to prepare fruit for apple butter boilings
and for drying into "snits"—apple slices sun dried on shed roofs
or large rocks. Snits were often traded for supplies at the general
store.*

An old-timer identified this artifact as part of a coffee mill.
  *Coffee—along with sugar, salt, and kerosene—was one of the
few staples the self-sufficient mountain people had to buy. If they
ran out of coffee, they would burn corn kernels and grind them
for a substitute.*
  *At butchering time the women sometimes used a coffee mill to
grind the sage used to season sausage.*

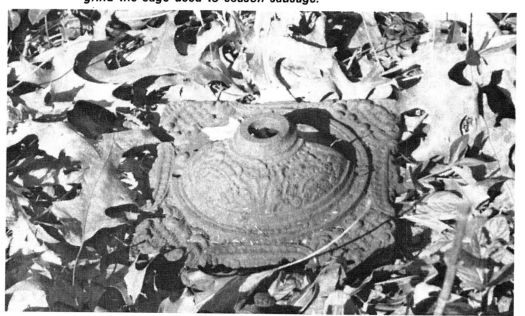

The mountain people bought sewing machines from traveling salesmen or through the Sears catalog.

Bits of decorative glassware and china provide evidence that the mountain woman had some possessions other than the bare necessities.

Whole crocks or jugs can be reassembled from the shards that litter some abandoned sites.

The rusting barrel hoops found at some sites are all that remain of an important commodity. Barrels were used to store flour, cornmeal, and sometimes kraut or a winter's supply of salt herring. Mountain orchardists shipped their fruit in them, too, and moonshiners needed barrels for their operations.

At stave mills throughout the Park area, workers cut and bundled barrel staves and hauled them out in mule wagons. When the staves were assembled into barrels, hoops made of wood or metal held them in place.

A bell's metallic clang once led children to the family milk cow and helped herdsmen locate the cattle or goats that were in their charge.

Today, Big Meadows is the only expanse of open land in Shenandoah. Fifty years ago, however, more of the Park was pasture than forest. A wide stretch of land between Fishers Gap and Milam Gap, the Loft Mountain and Simmons Gap areas, the Price lands near the Pinnacle, the Spitler "ranch" south of Skyland, and acreage in the Beahms Gap region were all cattle range. And nearly 1500 acres on the flat below Hogback was a goat farm.

Outsiders referred to making moonshine as "the local industry" in the Blue Ridge. Evidence of stills can be found near constant streams in out-of-the-way spots. This condensing coil, or worm, lies beside a spring deep in a hollow where excellent peach brandy as well as whiskey was produced.

Early vintage cars lie abandoned along old roads and at some homesites in the Park.

Old car buffs can marvel at wooden wheel spokes, gravity flow gas tanks, and carbide headlamps while they speculate on make and model and date of manufacture.

You frequently can find metal wagon tires along the steepest and rockiest of the Park's abandoned roads.

With their still-remaining wooden parts, this pair of wagon wheel hubs is a rare discovery!

The abandoned toy of a child now long grown adds to the poignancy one feels when exploring an old home site.

This metal truck and a tiny wagon found at one farm, a push toy at another site, and a small metal wheel at still another are lingering evidence that some mountain children had store-bought toys.

Part III

Cemeteries

Cemeteries

"Last weekend we added another cemetery to our collection—a real gem." A sentence like that could be a conversation stopper!

The cemeteries we collect are old mountain graveyards that we find on off-the-trail hikes in Shenandoah National Park. Sometimes we set out to find a particular cemetery we have read of or heard reference to. More often we make a chance discovery on a bushwhack hike.

We add a cemetery to our growing collection by marking the location on our map, noting pertinent details, and photographing the grave markers.

Some of the Park's cemeteries, though lovely, are not collector's items. They are visible from popular trails and even casual hikers know about them. It is the "rare" ones that have the most value to us— the ones that are not mentioned in any Park records, the ones that even our fellow bushwhackers have never found.

"Greenbriar" Cemetery is an example of one of these. Returning from a hike along an abandoned road we saw a haze of pale green in the winter woods. A closer look showed masses of greenbriar growing in a rectangular area with occasional fence posts standing along the perimeter.

"I'll bet that's a cemetery!" Jack exclaimed. We began to work our way around the dense growth, looking for a place where we could penetrate the barbed wire-like vines. The shady, uphill side was less of a tangle, and we inched along, freeing ourselves from the thorns every few steps.

Sure enough—mountain boulders and slabs of native rock set about six feet apart nearly covered the enclosed area. Some of the slabs were carved with names or with initials and dates: E.A. Atkins, 1893; J.M.B., May 2, 1888.

One of our favorite cemeteries is "Singlestone." A hiking friend who knew of our hobby asked us to accompany him and give our opinion as to whether "an interesting slab of rock" he had found on a recent bushwhacking expedition was a grave marker. He thought it looked like one, but it stood alone in the forest, far from any cabin site.

Of course we went. After a lengthy cross-country hike our friend announced, "There it is!"

We looked. "Which one is *it*?" I asked. For there on the nearly level mountain top were row after row of gray slabs. Most were spaced six feet or so apart, but here and there the symmetry was broken by smaller graves. We tried to count the plots but gave up and instead estimated the size of the burial ground as over an acre.

Grave markers in the mountain cemeteries we have found vary from uncut boulders and chiseled slabs of native stone to purchased memorials—some so weathered you can barely read the 19th century epitaphs, some of more recent vintage. Spring bulbs still bloom in family plots, and boxwood and periwinkle lend their green all year.

Collecting cemeteries may be an unusual hobby, but it isn't a morbid one. It's rather nice to sit awhile with the folks whose cabins we've discovered and whose orchard or spring we enjoyed down the old road a way.

Cemeteries usually were fenced. A few had decorative wrought iron fencing, but most were enclosed with wire strung between posts.

A few cemeteries that are accessible from Skyline Drive are still in active use. Family members visit the graves regularly, bringing bouquets of plastic flowers.

A long-forgotten hilltop cemetery with row after row of vertical slabs for grave markers covers more than an acre in a remote area of the Park. These dead rest in anonymity; none of the markers is inscribed.

Sometimes the native stone markers have names or initials and dates carved on them. Occasionally they bear only dates: "In a family plot you didn't have to put the initials if you had the date. People would know by the date who was buried there."

Grave markers like this were cut by tapping with an old chisel: "You had to choose the right kind of rock so it wouldn't shatter, and you had to know how hard to tap."

Metal markers provided by the funeral parlor are hidden in the periwinkle that carpets this mountain cemetery.

CHRISTINE LAM
DAUGHTER OF
JESSE & LEONA
LAM
AUG. 9, 1931
T BUD OF LOV

Imagine finding this memorial stone deep in the forest! Often infants' graves can be identified only by the short distance between pairs of mountain boulders.

The lettering was traced on this molded concrete marker while the cement was still soft.

The cemetery where Emily Dwyer lies is surrounded by a stone fence and bordered by rows of Norway maples brought in as nursery stock early in the century.

Once-whitewashed wooden slabs with letters and numbers snipped from tin mark a nineteenth century couple's graves.

The almost indiscernible epitaph on this turn-of-the-century stone reads:

> We have lost our darling mother,
> She has bid us all adieux,
> She has gone to live in heaven
> And her person is lost to sight.

Near the mother's grave is a homemade bench, inviting quiet contemplation.

Part IV

Along the Way

Along the Way

"Wait up! You're walking so fast we don't have time to see anything!" I puffed.

"What is there to see besides a lot of trees and rocks? Come on!" urged our hiking companion.

"Listen, there's a lot to see along the trails here in Shenandoah besides trees and rocks, but that's as good a place as any to start looking. You can tell what it was like when the mountain people lived here if you really look at the trees."

"Oh, oh; I can tell I'm about to hear a lecture on your favorite topic."

I ignored that.

"When you see a huge, spreading tree like that one over there with all the smaller trees around it, you can tell that you're walking through what used to be pasture land. That spreading tree grew up in the open without having to compete for light, and it shaded the cows that grazed here."

"It's hard to imagine that this woods was ever a pasture," he mused.

"Even the kinds of trees you see can tell you about the area's past," Jack instructed. "Pines are some of the first to grow up on cleared land. That pine forest we walked through earlier was probably somebody's corn field fifty years ago. You know, if you're good at identifying trees, you can sometimes tell you're near an old homesite because you spot a species that's not native to this region. The mountain people planted Norway spruce, arbor-vitae, white and gray poplar, Norway maple, silver maple, and even the paulownia, or 'princess tree', as ornamentals on their property."

"Trees are just trees to me, green in spring and summer, pretty colors in the fall, and bare all winter."

"But surely you can recognize an apple tree," I interrupted, exasperated. "That's definitely a sign you're near a homesite. . . . Look at those old gray stumps on the left. They're chestnut, from the days before the blight when lumbering and gathering tanbark were important to the mountain economy. Hey, maybe if we're lucky, we'll see the stump of a deadened tree."

"A 'deadened' tree?"

That spark of interest started me off again. "That's a tree that was girdled with an ax to kill it so sunlight could get to the ground under it."

"Why didn't the people just cut the tree down?"

"Sometimes they were in a hurry to get a crop in, and deadening the trees was quicker than cutting them down. Later, when they had time, they'd clear out the dead trees and use the wood for fences or fuel or whatever."

"And the rocks? What can we learn about the mountain people from them?"

"Well, we've already passed the rockpiles some farmer made when he cleared his land for planting or pasture, and we showed you a stone fence—"

"But what about the plain, ordinary rocks?" he teased.

"Listen, if you are really observant, 'plain, ordinary rocks' may turn out to be neither plain nor ordinary. Someday we'll take you to see some of the graffiti rocks we've found—rocks where the mountain people carved their names and sometimes even chiseled pictures of houses or cars."

"They must have had a lot of time on their hands."

"Well, what would you have done if you had no books or only a few of them, and if you had no phone or radio or TV, and if going to town was half a day's walk, and—"

"Okay, okay!" he interrupted. "I get the picture. . . . Listen, I think I'll go on ahead and meet you folks back at the car. That way I can get in some extra distance and you two can poke along as much as you please."

When we rejoined our friend later, he'd covered three or four miles more than we had. But he'd missed the two-story chimney just fifty feet off the trail, he hadn't seen the gate post with one hinge still attached, and he'd passed right by the faint abandoned road we followed to a partially standing cabin.

You might even say that we traveled further than he did, too, for we made a trip into the past. In our few miles of walking we went back in time more than five decades to see "the way it used to be."

Shenandoah National Park has more old roads than you could follow in a lifetime: major routes, deeply worn and rock-edged . . . logging and tanbark roads, twisting through an area dotted with chestnut stumps . . . wagon roads, with their twin furrows ending at a homesite. . . .

In some places the route of the old Spotswood Trail through Swift Run Gap is still wide open; elsewhere it is badly overgrown. Scores of mountain families lived along this well traveled trans-mountain road.

Mileage markers measured the traveler's progress along the Spotswood Trail.

Periwinkle—also called myrtle—grows in dooryards and cemeteries. If you see this evergreen ground cover, look for other signs of the mountain people's presence nearby.

Burdock, a weed with high nitrogen requirements, often grows up in abandoned barnyards and pig lots. A thick stand of burdock in a small, contained area is sometimes a clue to the presence of a farm.

This spring garden—a mountain woman's legacy—still blooms on Big Meadows each April.

Shrubs and flowers of many kinds beautified the mountain people's yards. Deep in the forest you may find boxwood, lilac, forsythia; a myriad of flowering bulbs; bridal wreath spirea, old-fashioned snowball bushes, and tangles of yellow roses.

The deep cut around the base of this stump was made when the tree was "deadened".

Miles and miles of split rail fences snake their way through the forest. Some once separated large tracts of land owned by valley farmers who grazed their cattle in mountain pastures.

Mountain people were hired by the land owners to maintain the fences and salt the herds.

Loose rails were laid between these posts to serve as a gate that required no hinges, latch, or other metal parts. Gates like these were common where roads crossed fence lines. Dooryard gates usually were of the hinged variety.

This chest-high stone fence along an old roadside is an excellent example of the masonry skill of the mountain farmer.

"My father built stone fences when he was a young man," recalls a former resident of the area. "He used a string to lay out a straight line, and he had a wooden frame that tapered some at the top. He filled the frame with rocks—big ones at the bottom and smaller ones higher up."

Lumber companies owned large tracts of mountain land and bought timber rights to additional acreage. Huge piles of slab wood still mark the sites of some of the itinerant sawmills that operated in the Park area during the early '30s.

Sometimes the slab wood was used by the mountain people to make cowsheds or woodsheds. Two slabs were stood vertically and a third was nailed over the space between them in forming the walls. The roofs of these three-sided buildings also were constructed by overlapping slabs.

When the mountain people left the Park area they were not allowed to take any parts of their buildings or fences from their farms. The government planned to recycle these materials in the homesteads being built for families who lacked the resources to relocate on their own. But the rusty rolls of wire you see here, and others throughout the Park, testify that the plan was not always carried out.

Tracing a tangle of telephone wire to an insulator in the middle of the woods comes as a surprise! A few prosperous families had phones, and in some communities there was a telephone in the general store.

Today's youth spray-paint their graffiti, emblazoning slogans or the names of rock groups more often than their own names. In contrast, the mountain people painstakingly carved their names and dates in stone. O. Fox—and countless others—carved a record on this boulder along the roadside in the early days of the century.

The width of the long-ago knife marks on this beech is a measurement of the time that has passed since WJW and MMB traveled the old road along the river from their hollow to town.

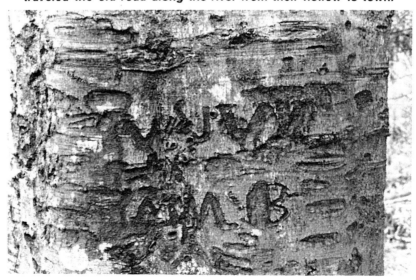

A Last Word

We have found more than 300 sites in Shenandoah—farms, mills, schools, churches, cemeteries—and each discovery has been accompanied by mounting excitement.

Fence remnants alert our senses. Gnarled apple trees quicken the pulse. Periwinkle spreading along the forest floor slows our steps ... and there ahead of us, blending into the dappled woods, we see a crumbling cabin.

The day's first challenge has been met. Through good woodsmanship and careful observation, we've found the site. The next challenge is intellectual. We must reconstruct in our mind's eye how this farm looked when the jumble of rocks and timber was a house; those locust woods beyond, a field; the rusted artifacts, utensils in daily use.

The final challenge is a spiritual one: to attune ourselves to the people who lived and worked and, perhaps, died here half a century or more ago. And sometimes when we've admired the craftsmanship in the stonework of chimneys and fences, handled often-used tools or kitchenware, and traced the faint lettering on mossy gravestones, we feel we know these faceless people better than our own ancestors whose faded photographs show us but an isolated moment in their lives.